Dwayne's Guitar Lessons Presents:

Learn To Play Lead Guitar

By

Guitar Teacher
Dwayne Jenkins

Introduction

Learn To Play Lead Guitar is for the student who is well versed in playing rhythm guitar, and wants to take their playing to the next level by learning how to play guitar solos.

The student should already have a basic understanding of playing chords, creating chord progressions, and guitar riffs, and reading basic music notation such as guitar tabs.

With this fundamental foundation already in place, you will be able to progress faster at becoming a lead guitarist. You'll just need the desire to learn.

Playing lead guitar is an exciting and rewarding expression of your inner passion for the guitar. With this skill, you can add a unique voice to the music while increasing your mastery of the fretboard.

But for you to do that, you will need to master a few techniques, such as learning scales, phrasing, and knowing where to play a solo in a song. As this knowledge will allow you to stay in key, and sound good with every note.

Scales such as the pentatonic and blues scales will be recommended to start as they are widely popular with many different styles of music.

Daily practice of such techniques as hammer-ons, pull-offs, bends, slides, and vibrato will build finger dexterity and independence. Along with allowing you to add emotion to your playing and bring the scales to life.

You will also learn to set goals, develop a practice routine, and get tips on playing by ear. Along with learning guitar solos from recordings. This will guide you on how to create a unique style of your own.

It is all here in this book Learn To Play Lead Guitar. A comprehensive training guide that will teach you to develop the skill of playing awesome guitar solos and melody lines.

Developing your unique signature style is what playing guitar is all about. Especially playing lead guitar. This book will show you how in a very simple step-by-step method.

So get the book, get started on the journey, and let your passion for playing guitar solos shine through as I guide you along the way.

Dwayne Jenkins

Table of Contents

Chapter 1 Lead Guitar Basics

Lesson 1: The scale of five notes

When it comes to playing lead guitar, I recommend you start with the scale of five notes. The pentatonic scale. This is the most common scale to play guitar solos in. The reason for this is that it works with music of many different styles.

Penta means five and tonic means tones or notes. So it means a scale of five tones or a scale of five notes. Pentatonic. There are both major and minor pentatonic scales. These are what we are going to study in this training course.

Since all the great guitar players (Hendrix, Page, Clapton, etc) use them for their solos, it only makes sense to learn them. This will not only help you with creating your own guitar solos but also understand the ones that they have created.

If ever in the future you decide you want to learn one of their songs, you will understand how the solo is constructed and thus be able to learn it easier and quicker. This will make playing it more enjoyable.

In the regular musical alphabet, there are twelve notes. This is sometimes called the chromatic scale. Out of these twelve notes, we take seven notes to create the major scale. We then take five notes out of the seven to make the pentatonic scale.

Chromatic scale = 12 notes

Major scale = 7 notes

Pentatonic scale = 5 notes.

These five notes are a magical formula we can use for playing guitar solos and melody lines. We can also use them for creating guitar riffs. It is for this reason that the pentatonic scale is so popular and universal.

There is a lot that can be taught about this scale. But for our purposes here in this training, we'll keep it simple. We'll look at the major pentatonic and minor pentatonic. These scales will allow you to play over any chord progression in any key.

Let's look at these in a bit more detail.

Each scale and chord no matter what type it is has a musical formula. A major triad (3 note chord) is a 1 3 5 formula and the minor triad is a 1 flat 3 5 formula. This is very important to know for a better understanding of the pentatonic scale.

As I mentioned before, the major scale has 7 notes and the pentatonic scale has 5 notes. So what we do is we take 5 notes out of the 7 from the major scale. It is for this reason they work together in harmony.

Let's use the key of C major as an example:

C major: C D E F G A B
          1 2 3 4 5 6 7

C major pentatonic: C D E G A
                     1 2 3 5 6

Can you see how we just take 5 notes out of the C major scale to make the C major pentatonic scale? Since these notes come from the key of C major, they will work in harmony. Chords and melody can both be created from the same key.

This works with the minor pentatonic scale as well.

Lesson 2: The minor pentatonic scale

Like the major pentatonic scale formula, there is also a minor pentatonic scale formula. This one also uses notes out of its major counterpart. Let's look at an example in C as we did before to see this in more detail.

The key of C major: C D E F G A B
                      1 2 3 4 5 6 7

Since this is a minor scale, we will flatten the 3rd note. Just like in a minor chord. A major chord has a natural 3rd and a minor chord has a flattened third. The same goes for scales. In this case, we will also add a flattened 7th note.

C minor pentatonic: C Eb F G Bb
                     1 b3 4 5 b7

As you can see, we still use 5 notes, but we don't use the 6th and flatten the 3rd and 7th notes of the scale.

In the major pentatonic scale, we use the 1 2 3 5 & 6th notes.
In the minor pentatonic scale, we use the 1 b3 4 5 & b7th notes.

Learn these two scale formulas well as they will be the foundation of your lead guitar playing.

When it comes to playing lead guitar, the first place to start will be the minor pentatonic. The reason for this is that it works over any chord progression in a minor key. But it can also work over progressions in major keys as well.

It is a very simple scale to learn and has a multitude of applications. That is why it will be the first scale we will learn about. This scale along with the major pentatonic will become the foundation of your lead guitar playing.

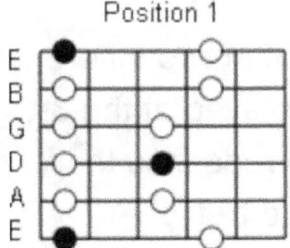

Position 1

This is referred to as the minor pentatonic scale box pattern. The reason for this is because of the way the notes line up across the fretboard. This makes them easy to learn and easy to play.

Once you learn this box pattern, you then learn to play it in different places along the fretboard. This will change the key in which you play in.

6

Here are some examples of what I'm talking about.

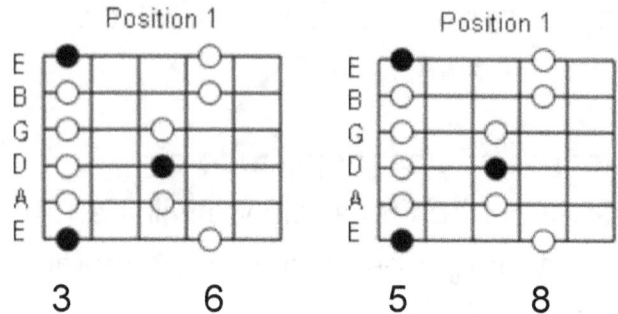

Here is an example of the same box pattern but in two different positions along the fretboard. The first one is played at the 3rd fret. This would be in the key of G minor. The reason is that the root of the scale (the G) is located at the 3rd fret.

The second one is played at the 5th fret and would indicate the key of A minor. Once again, because the root of the scale (the A) is located at the 5th fret. As you can see, it's the same pattern, just a different location.

This is why it would be a good idea to memorize your fretboard along with this minor pentatonic box pattern. It will allow you to determine where to play in any particular minor key that you are presented with very quickly.

Lesson 3: The major pentatonic scale

The major pentatonic scale is very much the same thing. Although it is a different box pattern, the concept is the same. You learn the pattern and determine where to play it in any given major key.

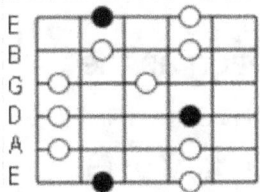

Since this is a major pentatonic scale, the notes will be lined up differently than the minor. This makes it a different pattern. But it provides the same concept. The darkened notes are the root notes of the scale.

Knowing these is important because it will help you to find starting and stopping points when creating guitar licks. Which is what guitar solos are made of. More on this later. For now, just learn the major pentatonic scale box pattern.

Let's take a look at these in different positions like we did the minor pentatonic scale.

Here is the major pentatonic scale across the fretboard in different locations.

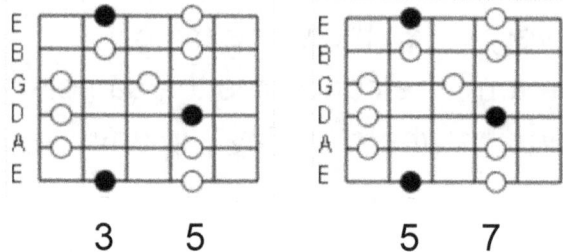

As you can see, I present these in the same location as the minor pentatonic scales. In G and A. The difference is, that here you would be playing in the major keys. The key of G major and the key of A major.

Notice how this pattern looks different from the minor. Different, yes, more difficult? No. If you think in patterns when it comes to learning the guitar, it will make it a lot easier to understand concepts and techniques.

Learn this pattern after you master the minor. Play it up and down the fretboard and think about what major key you're playing in. At the 7th fret would be what key? Tenth fret?

As we go through the training, you'll discover how to bring these scales and others to life and sound like music.

Lesson 4: Hammer-ons and pull-offs

Once you have those two scale patterns down and can play them up and down the neck at any fret, you want to learn hammer-ons and pull-offs. These two things are the most common technique when playing lead guitar.

A hammer-on is when you pick a note and hammer-on to the next note. A pull-off is the opposite. You pick a note and you pull-off to the note behind it. A hammer-on is like adding and a pull-off is like subtracting.

Once you get these techniques down individually, you will learn to put them together to create music with your pentatonic guitar scales.

Let's look at these in more detail.

As you can see, the hammer-on adds a note as where the pull-off, takes one away. The numbers will indicate which one is being played.

In the hammer-on example, you place your index finger on the 5th fret and hammer-on to the 7th with your ring finger, In the case of the pull-off, you place two fingers down at the same time and pull-off the 7th fret back to the 5th fret.

Practice these two motions until you have this concept down. Once you have the hammer-on down, try it on other strings.

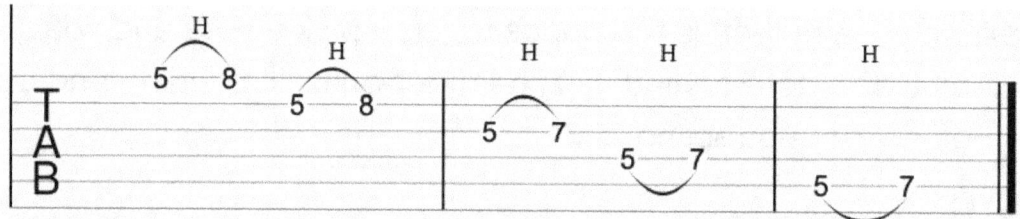

Here we go through the A minor pentatonic scale with hammer-ons. This is a great exercise and a way to master hammer-ons on different strings.

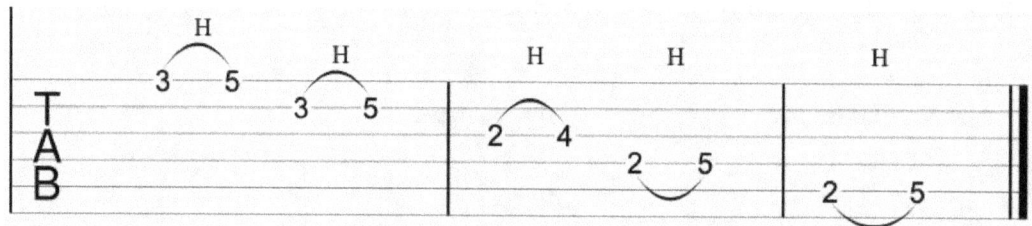

Here is the same example with the G major pentatonic. Master the technique and work with it daily.

This will allow you to master both the technique and the scales at the same time.

Let's take a look at pull-offs. We want to do the same with these. To execute these properly you place two fingers down on the same string. (unless you're pulling off to an open string) and pick the first note while pulling off to the one behind it.

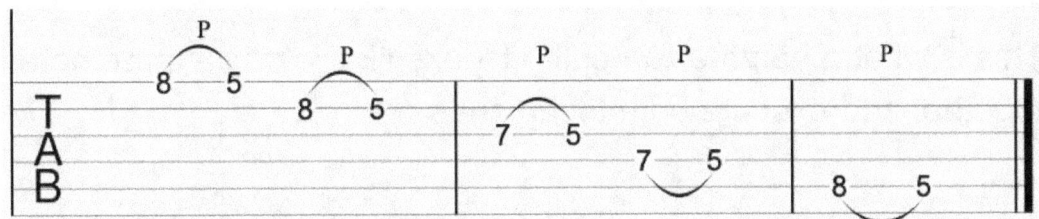

Here we have the same thing as before. Except they are pull-offs instead of hammer-ons. Work with these slowly and get them down. Listen to how familiar they sound when you play them.

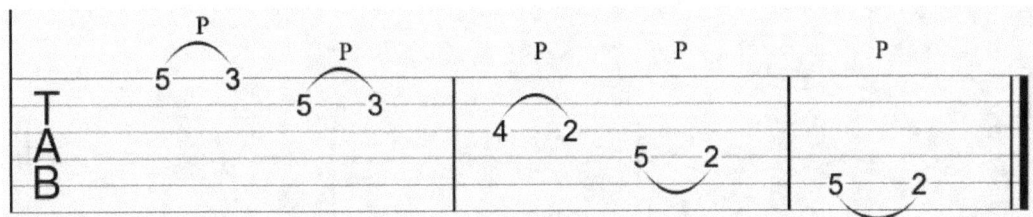

Here we have pull-offs in the G major pentatonic scale. The pull-offs on the 4th and 5th strings are a bit of a stretch but will make a good exercise for your fingers.

Once you have these down individually, work on combining them for additional musical creativity.

12

Let's take a look at some examples of playing them together.

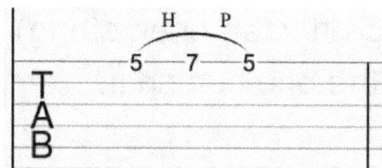

This is what a hammer-on pull-off looks like. You tie three notes together and execute both techniques.

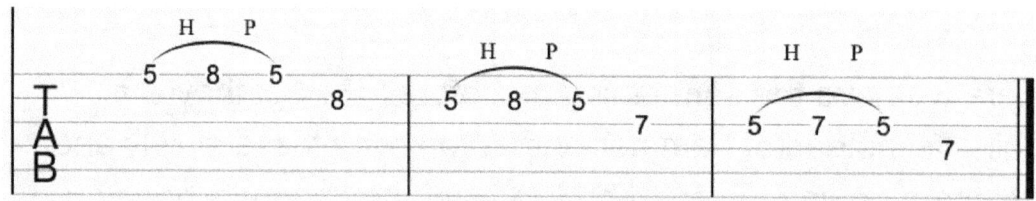

Here we have this technique utilized in the A minor pentatonic scale over the first four strings.

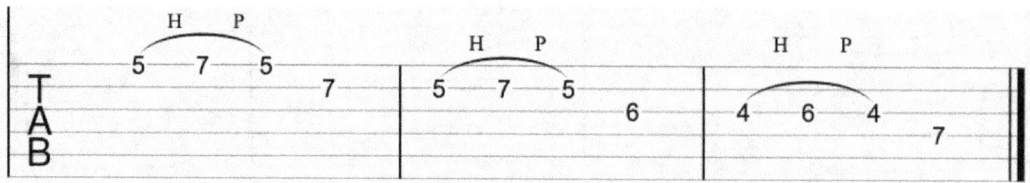

Same thing here. Hammer-ons and pull-offs in the A major pentatonic scale.

Work on these in the G major and minor pentatonic scales as well. The better you know these the better you'll sound.

Lesson 5: Chapter 1 Quiz

In this lesson, I have taught you some basic fundamental principles of playing lead guitar. Now comes the part to see how well you learned the lessons.

If you're not too sure about an answer, no need to worry. They are all in this chapter. So just go back and find it.

Q: What is the pentaonic scale?

A: _____

Q: What two pentatonic scales are presented in this chapter?

A: _____

Q: What does pentatonic mean?

A: _____

Q: Why start with is particular scale?

A: _____

Q: How does it differ from the major scale?

A: _____

14

Q: What is the number formula for the major pentatonic scale?

A: _____

Q: What is the number formula for the minor pentatonic scale?

A: _____

Q: What is a hammer-on?

A: _____

Q: How do you write a hammer-on in notation?

A: _____

Q: What is a pull-off?

A: _____

Q: How do you write a pull-off in notation?

A: _____

Q: What is a hammer-on pull-off?

A; _____

Q: How do you write a hammer-on pull-off in notation?

A; _____

Know the answers to these questions, and know them well.
These will set the foundation of your lead guitar education. This
foundation will provide you with better lead guitar playing.

Chapter 1 Summary

In this first chapter, we have covered some basics of lead guitar playing. We start with the pentatonic scale. This is a scale of five notes commonly used worldwide.

We start with this scale because it is easy to learn, easy to use, and works great in all styles of music. We learned how it is different from the major scale and used by all the great lead guitar players.

We then learned about how the pentatonic scale can be both major and minor. This is great because we now have something that will work over any major or minor chord progression.

We then looked at hammer-ons and pull-offs. These are two techniques commonly used when playing guitar solos. They will set the foundation for your lead guitar licks when creating guitar solos in the future.

We then learn about how these techniques can be used together to make the pentatonic scales sound more musical. Master this fundamental concept and it'll set you up for future lead guitar concepts and techniques.

16

Chapter 2 Lead Guitar Licks

Lesson 6: Lead guitar bends

Now that you have the hammer-ons and pull-offs down it's time to add some other techniques common to playing guitar solos. The first one that we will look at is string bends. Where you play a note and bend it to give it expression.

String bends are great because they work very well with the hammer-ons and pull-offs that you learned in the last chapter.

Here is an example of a string bend:

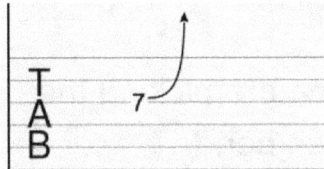

In this example, you pick the 7th note on the third string and bend it up. I know in the notation it shows down, but in reality, you bend it up toward the ceiling.

This is a technique commonly used in a lot of different styles of guitar playing. You simply pick a note (any note) and bend it. What this does, is it gives expression to the note and makes it sound musical.

18

String bends are a great way to express notes. Let's look at how we can use this awesome technique in addition to what we have already learned.

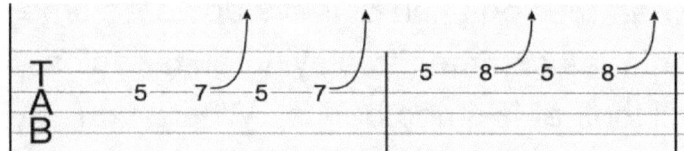

Here are string bends from the A minor pentatonic scale. I recommend you use two fingers when bending the 8th fret on the second string.

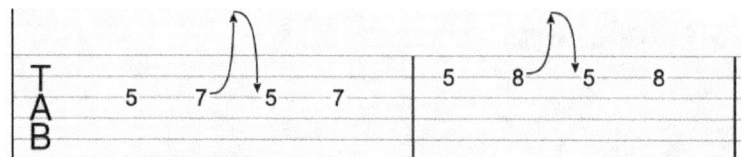

Here we bend the string and then release it before picking the next note. This gives us two notes out of each bend.

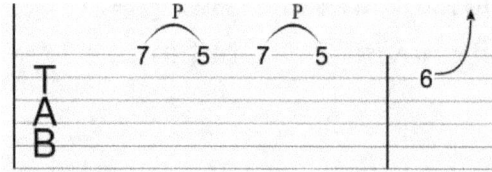

Here is an example of using two pull-offs and a bend.

Use hammer-ons, pull-offs, and bends together along with the pentatonic scales, and see what you come up with.

Lesson 7: Lead guitar slides

Sliding from note to note is another great way to express the notes within the pentatonic scales. This technique incorporates you picking a note and sliding up or down to another note.

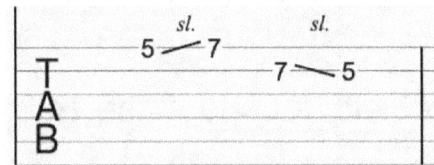

Here is an example of a slide up and a slide down. Slide up to the 7th fret on the first string, and slide down to the 5th fret on the second string.

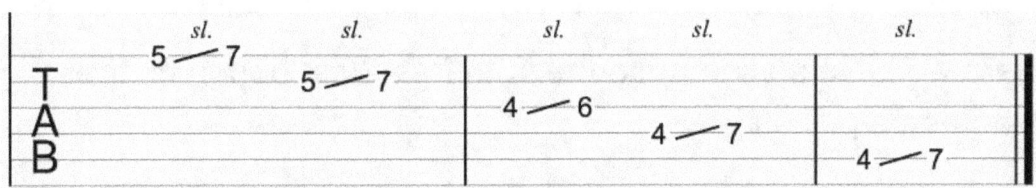

Here we have slides that ascend through the A major pentatonic scale. Get this down and then do this with the minor.

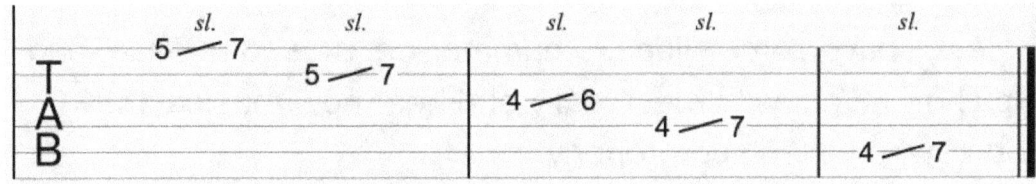

Here is an example of sliding down through the scale.

There are many different ways to slide notes. Single, or double, you just need to be creative. Now that we know what a slide is and how to do it, let's add it to the licks we already know.

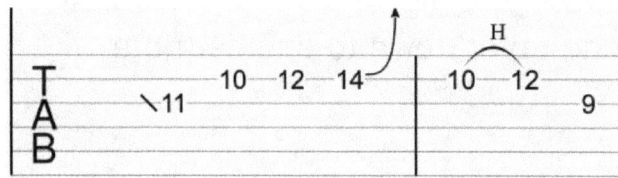

Here we have a slide up to the 11th fret with a bend at the 14th and a hammer-on at the 10th.

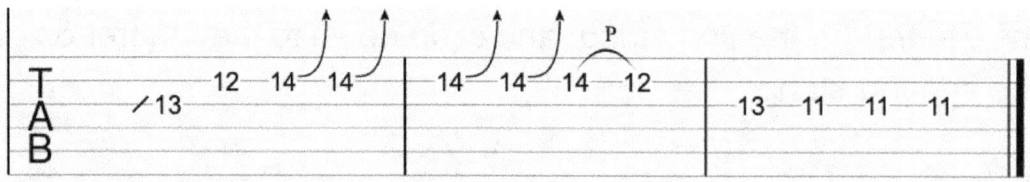

Here we have a slide up to the 13th fret a few bends on the 14th and a pull off.

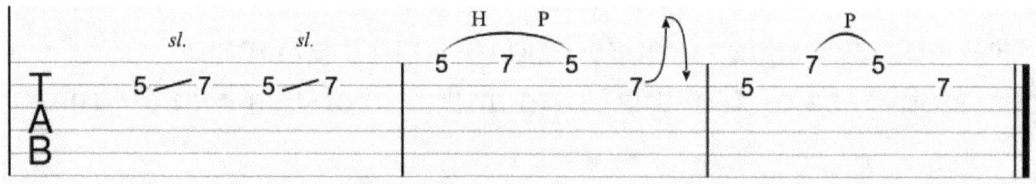

Here we have some slides, a hammer-on, a bend release, and a pull-off. Work with these daily and hear how musical they sound when executed properly.

Lesson 8: Lead Guitar Vibrato

We now come to a technique that is vital to master. Vibrato.
This is where you bend the string slightly up and down to mimic
a singer's vibrato in their voice.

Here is an example of vibrato. We pick the 5th fret of the first
string and bend it slightly up and down.

Here we have vibrato being played on different frets on different
strings throughout the A major pentatonic scale.

Same thing here except it's through the minor pentatonic scale.
Work on mastering this technique.

Now that we understand how to execute vibrato, let's use it with our other cool lead guitar techniques.

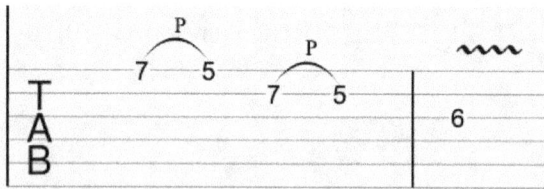

Here we have two pull-offs and a vibrato in the the A major pentatonic scale.

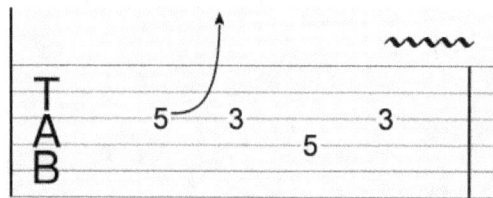

Here we start with a bend and end with vibrato. Vibrato is a great way to end a musical phrase.

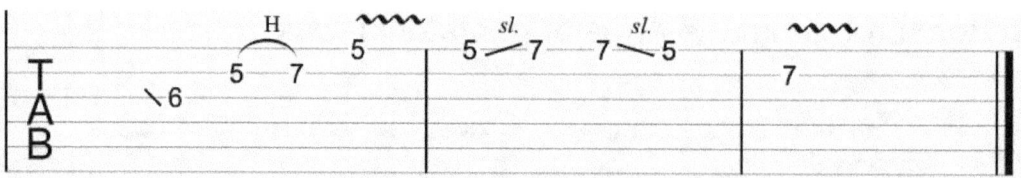

Here we have some slides, a hammer-on, and some vibrato. All out of the major pentatonic scale.

Vibrato is not an easy technique to master, but with dedication to daily practice, you'll soon get it to sound great!

Lesson 9: Lead Guitar Trills

Trills are a great technique to have in your lead guitar toolbox. They are when you play a hammer-on pull-off repeatedly. This is a great way to add stamina and strength to your fingers.

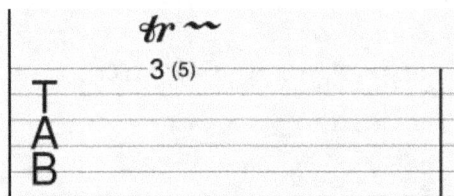

Here we have a trill on the 3rd fret of the first string. A hammer-on to the 5th fret that is continuously repeated.

These can be played all over the fretboard and are commonly found in a lot of guitar songs. Once you get the technique down you'll begin to hear it when you listen to music.

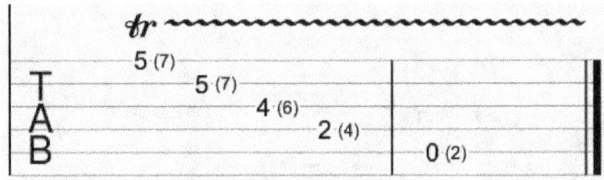

Here are some trills throughout the fretboard on different strings. Notice the last one is an open trill to the 2nd fret.

Work with these and get them down.

24

Now let's add these to the other licks that we've learned.

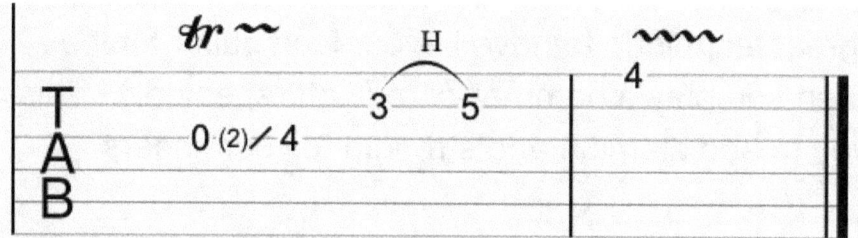

Here we start with an open trill and slide up to the 4th fret. Then add a hammer-on and end with vibrato.

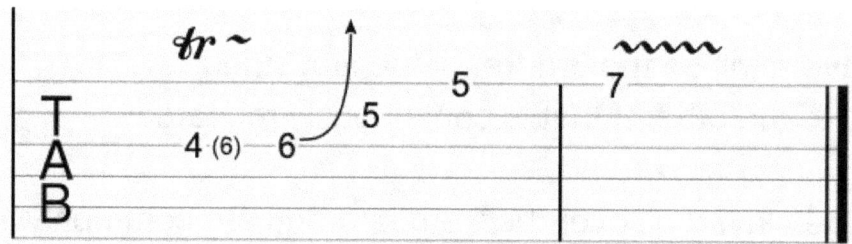

Here we start with a trill at the 4th fret, bend up on the 6th, and add a vibrato at the end.

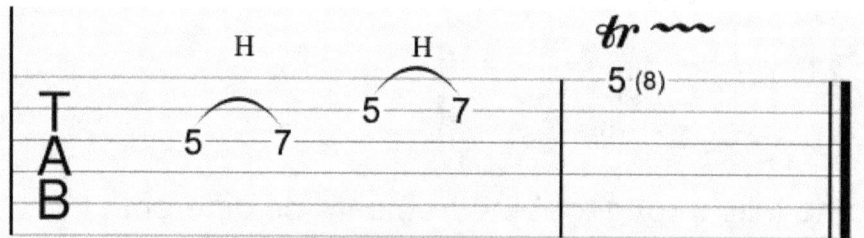

Here are a couple of hammer-ons and a trill. Work with these examples and see what you can create on your own.

Lesson 10: Chapter 2 Quiz

Now we have a simple test for chapter two. Once again, this is to make sure you know the material well.

If you don't know the answer, go back and look through the lesson. All answers will be found there.

Q: What is a string bend?

A: _____

Q: What is a string bend release?

A: _____

Q: What is a guitar slide?

A: _____

Q: What two directions can you slide in?

A: _____

Q: What is vibrato?

A: _____

Q: What techniques are used in the 2nd example on page 18?
A: _____

Q: What techniques are used in the 3rd example on page 20?
A: _____

Q: What techniques are used in the 1st example on page 22?
A: _____

Q: What techniques are used in the 3rd example on page 24?
A: _____

Q: What techniques are used in the 2nd example on page 20?
A: _____

Q: What techniques are used in the 3rd example on page 18?
A: _____

Q: Why are these techniques so important to learn?
A: _____

This chapter of personality traits will be the foundation of your lead guitar playing. So I suggest you spend some time mastering it.

Chapter 2 Summary

In chapter two you have learned about building a solid foundation for playing lead guitar. You learned techniques such as string bends, slides, vibrato, and trills.

You also learned how these are written in tab notation. This will add to your reading skills. Learn to execute these for better overall musicianship.

But for this to happen, you need to practice them daily. Work with these techniques. Understand the concept of what they are and how they bring the scales to life.

These simple techniques can be played on any scale in any key. They are found in all guitar solos and should be in yours as well if you decide to write your own.

They will also help you in learning guitar solos from your favorite guitar players. Just start with them in the order you've been taught. You will soon be sounding like a lead guitarist.

In the beginning, this is not easy because the muscles in your fingers will need to be developed. But with daily practice of this chapter, they will. And that is when the true fun begins.

28

Chapter 3 All 5 Pentatonic Scales

Lesson 11: Scale patterns 1 & 2

Regarding the pentatonic scale, we can create 5 different scale patterns. These 5 different scale patterns will span the whole fretboard and give us a roadmap to work with.

This is very beneficial because once we master this roadmap, we will know exactly how to get to where we want to go in a solo.

More importantly, we will be able to stay in musical key in the process. This is something I see a lot of students of lead guitar playing have a problem with.

Let's now take a review of the two scale patterns learned so far. Pattern one and pattern two. These two patterns alone would allow you to play any solo you want.

They can be played individually in both minor and major, or combined to play in both minor and major.

I say minor first because most Rock and Blues guitar is in a minor key. It is what gives it its sound and emotion.

Pentatonic pattern one:

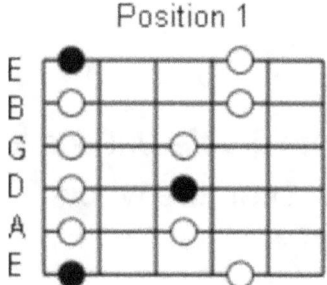

As you can see this is the minor pentatonic scale. It is called position 1 because of what I mentioned before about most songs in Rock & Blues being in a minor key.

Pentatonic pattern two:

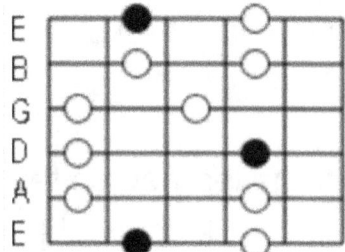

This is pattern two. Since there are 5 notes, we can create 5 different patterns. Master these first two patterns and get to where you can play them all over the fretboard.

As we progress through this chapter, we will learn all 5 patterns to create the ultimate fretboard roadmap.

Lesson 12: Scale Patterns 3 & 4

Each pattern is based on a note that is in the scale. For example, if we are playing the pentatonic scales in the key of A minor our notes would be:

A C D E G

Each pattern would start on one of these notes. Pattern 1 would start on A, pattern 2 would start on C, pattern 3 would start on D, pattern 4 would start on E, and pattern 5 would start on G.

What's great about these patterns is they always stay in the same order no matter what key you play them in. This means that once you learn them in one key, you can easily play them in any key.

You just need to master their shapes and locations within each key that you play them in. As you do, you will discover that each one has its character. This is because of the location of the notes within the scale pattern.

This will be what you want to master. All 5 scale patterns, and what you can create with each of them.

Here are the third and fourth scale patterns to master.

Pentatonic pattern three:

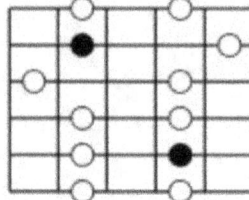

As you can see, this pattern is different from the other two. Although it uses the same notes.

Pentatonic pattern four:

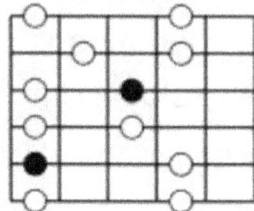

Once again we can see that the pattern has changed, but the notes stay the same.

Master these two pattern shapes like you did the first two. Then play them in different positions on the fretboard.

Lesson 13: Scale pattern 5

Now we come to the last one, pattern 5. As I mentioned before, once you learn all 5 you will create a fretboard roadmap that will allow you to go in any direction in any key and sound great!

Pentatonic pattern five:

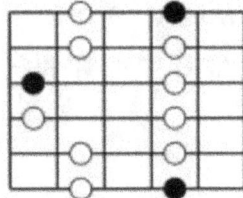

This is the final pattern to master. It is simple and easy to play. Get it down and play it in different positions on the fretboard.

All the great guitar players play these patterns in their solos. Once you master them, they will start to reveal themselves. But this won't come without daily practice.

Go over each one individually and get to know each one very well. You want to know these scale patterns as well as you know your guitar chords.

Think of these like you did the first 5 fundamental chords you learned for playing rhythm. Except these are for playing lead.

As I said, these can be played over minor and major chord progressions. You just need to keep them in order and know where to play them.

Since pattern 1 is a minor pentatonic scale, start with this one first and proceed through the other four when playing in a minor key like A minor.

Since pattern 2 is a major pentatonic scale, start with this one first and proceed through the other four when playing in a major key like C major.

If you take the time to learn these five scale patterns and unlock the mysteries that they hold within them, you will become a great lead guitar player.

It just comes down to study and practice daily. Most lead guitar players that you get inspired by have done this. They have committed to this training of these scales.

Once you get these down and know how to play them using the personality traits that I taught you previously, you'll sound like a true lead guitarist.

But you must commit to study and practice!

Pattern 1 in A minor

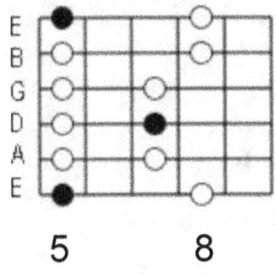

5   8

Pattern 2 in C major

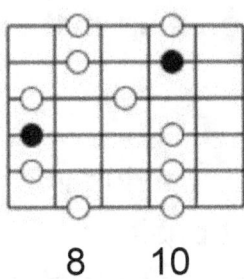

8   10

Pattern 2 in A minor

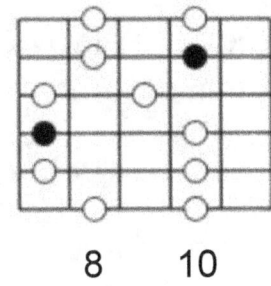

8   10

Pattern 3 in C major

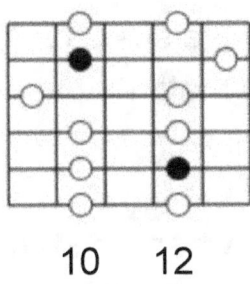

10   12

Pattern 3 in A minor

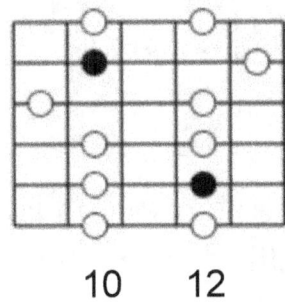

10   12

Pattern 4 in C major

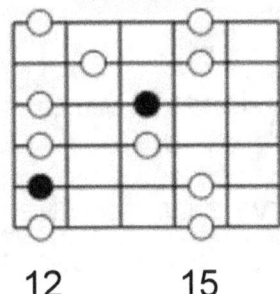

12   15

Can you see how you start with pattern 1 in a minor key and pattern 2 in a major key?

Notice how the next scale pattern starts where the previous one left off. If you're playing in A minor, you start at the 5th fret and end on the 8th. You then start pattern 2 on the 8th fret where pattern 1 left off.

The same thing goes for playing in a major key. Here you start with pattern 2 in the first position (because it is the major pentatonic scale) and proceed from there in the same fashion as you did with the minor key.

What is great about these scale patterns is that they are always in the same order. No matter what key (major or minor) you choose to play them in.

You just need to know where to start along the fretboard and the order in which they come in. This will not come overnight, but you will get it with daily practice.

Notice, I didn't include pattern 5? I did this so you could figure out where it would be located within these two keys.

If you follow the intervals of the other three patterns, you should be able to figure it out. Remember, the next pattern (no matter which of the 5 it is) always starts where the previous one left off.

Lesson 14: All 5 scale patterns

Now that we have learned all 5 scale patterns individually, let's look at them as a whole.

When playing a guitar solo over a chord progression in any minor key you would play the pentatonic scale patterns in this order.

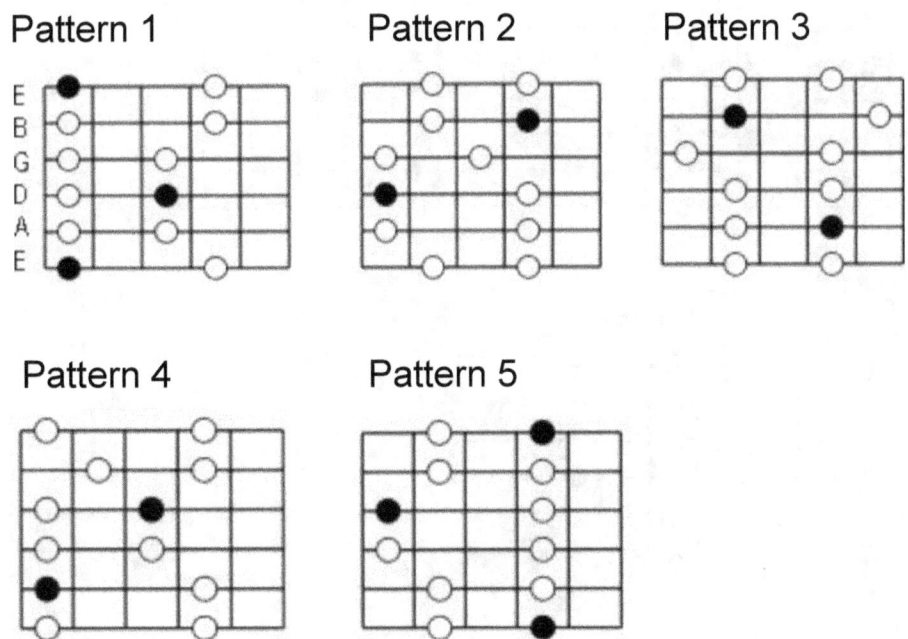

By playing them in this order, you will stay in key every time. You just need to know what fret to start at. This will depend on what minor key you are playing in.

38

The same thing goes when playing these scale patterns in a major key. Know what fret to start at, and what order they are played in.

When playing a guitar solo over a chord progression in any major key you would play the pentatonic scale patterns in this order.

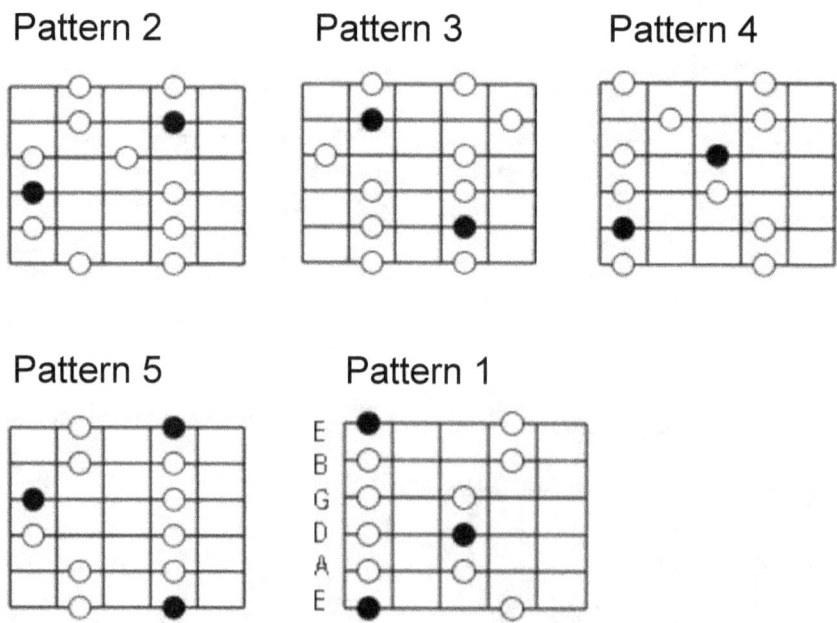

As you can see, we are still using the same 5 pentatonic scale patterns. The only difference is that when we solo over a major chord progression, we start with pattern 2 in the first position.

We do this because pattern 2 is the major pentatonic scale.

If you are playing a guitar solo in a minor key start with pattern 1 in the first position. If you are playing a guitar solo in a major key, start with pattern 2 in the first position.

The reason for this is because of the way the notes line up. If you'd like to know about this further in detail, I suggest you learn your notes along the fretboard and analyze the notes within the patterns.

If not, just memorize the patterns. It's up to you. Either way, I recommend you at least know your notes on the 6th string. This will inform you where to play these scale patterns in any major or minor key.

Example:

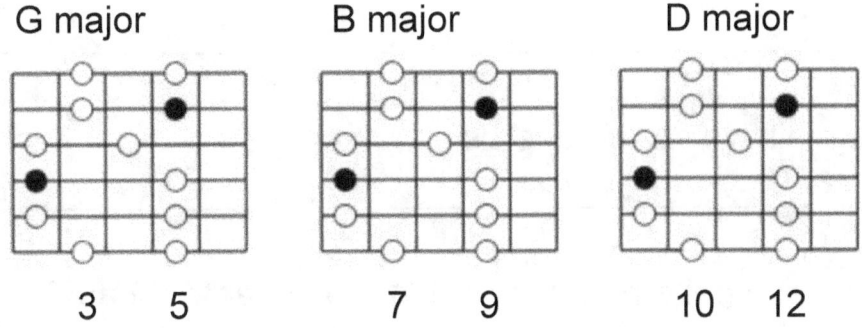

Notice how G, B, and D major use the same pattern but start at different locations on the fretboard.   This is why knowing your notes on the 6th string is very important.

Lesson 15:   Chapter 3 Quiz

In this chapter, we have learned all 5 pentatonic scale patterns. Knowing all five will enhance your overall musicianship. Along with the opportunity to play all along the fretboard in any key.

Q: Is pentatonic pattern 1 a major or minor scale?
A: _____

Q: Is pentatonic pattern 2 a major or minor scale?
A: _____

Q: What pattern would you start with in the key of G major?
A: _____

Q: How pattern would you start with in the key of A minor?
A: _____

Q: Why learn all five scale patterns?
A: _____

Q: What do these patterns create along the guitar fretboard?
A: _____

Make sure to study these scale patterns. Know exactly what order they are played in, and what fret to play them on.

Chapter 3 Summary

In chapter three we have learned all 5 pentatonic scales. These are essential tools that can take your guitar solos to the next level.

The objective is to know these scale patterns like the back of your hand. Know the order to play them, how they connect, and where to play them in any major or minor key.

Patterns 1 and 2 are the most important to master. This is because pattern 1 is the minor scale and pattern 2 is the major scale.

Although they can both be used in either case. It all comes down to where you play them along the fretboard. Knowing this will allow you the freedom to improvise.

The roadmap that these 5 patterns create spans the entire guitar neck. Learning all five will allow you to break out of patterns to explore more of the fretboard.

This will enhance your knowledge and understanding of lead guitar. It also keeps you from getting stuck playing just one or two patterns.

Each scale pattern has its own character. As you learn each one individually you will discover this. Pattern 3 has note intervals that are different from pattern 4.

Pattern 5 also has unique note intervals that give it character and emotion. This is why it is so important to learn all five. You bring out additional emotion that you might not otherwise.

Pick a minor key (B minor for instance) and go through the scale patterns individually in that key. Know exactly where the scale patterns reside in that key.

Do this also with any major key. Go through the patterns in the order presented. Visualize how they connect. Move between them on different strings.

Bring them to life with the personality traits you learned earlier. Do this enough and you'll soon sound like a true lead guitar player.

Chapter 4 The Blues Scale

Lesson 16: The minor blues scale

Another scale that is very popular with playing lead guitar is the blues scale. Which is the same thing as the pentatonic scale, except you add a note.

This additional note in the minor blues scale is the flat 5th note. This note gives the scale a darker, moodier sound. Perfect for playing the blues.

The minor pentatonic scale formula = 1 b3 4 5 b7
The minor blues scale formula = 1 b3 4 b5 5 b7

If we were playing in the key of A minor, the notes of the two scales would be:

The A minor pentatonic scale: A C   D E G
                               1 b3 4 5 b7

The A minor blues scale: A   C   D Eb E G
                          1   b3 4 b5 5 b7

See how simple this is?

The scale box pattern is the same except we now add the flat fifth note in two places. This does two things:

1. It gives the scale a new character
2. It extends the pattern for more playability.

Let's take a look at the difference:

Minor pentatonic scale.   Minor blues scale

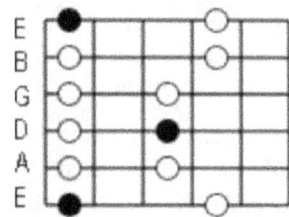   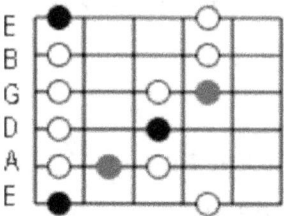

See how these two patterns are very similar? All we did was add the flat fifth (or blue note as it is sometimes called) to the scale.

Because of the note location, we can add it in a couple of places. This allows more flexibility with the scale and more creativity for our fingers.

Since you already know the minor pentatonic, all you have to do is add the blue note in two locations. Listen to how it changes the tone of the scale.

Lesson 17: The major blues scale

This same concept works with the major blues scale. Instead of adding the flat fifth note, we add the flat third note. It is this flat third note that gives its character.

Let's take a look at the two scale formulas.

The major pentatonic scale formula: 1 2 3 5 6
The major blues scale formula: 1 2 b3 3 5 6

If we were playing in the key of C major the notes of the two scales would be:

The C major pentatonic scale: C D E G A
                               1 2 3 5 6

The C major blues scale: C D Eb E G A
                          1 2 b3 3 5 6

Do you see how this concept is the same as the minor blues scale?

Study this formula and make sure you fully understand it. If it doesn't come to you at first keep working with it.

Let's take a look at the two box patterns.

Major pentatonic scale.   Major blues scale

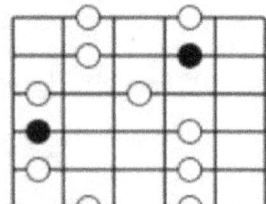 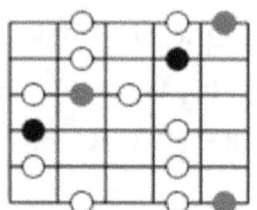

As you can see we can add the blue note (as they sometimes call it) in three different locations. A little different than the minor blues scale. Where it is added in only two places.

Look at how this additional note in the three locations allows for more creativity. Allows you to play three notes on some strings instead of the usual two.

This also works for the other three pentatonic scales.

Pattern 3   Pattern 4   Pattern5

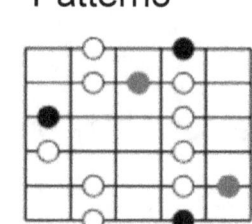

Master all 5 blues scale patterns for additional creativity.

Lesson 18: Major scale guitar licks

Now that we've learned some scales and personality traits (hammer-ons, pull-offs, bends, slides, etc) we want to put these elements together to create music.

These give you insight into how to use the strings to create solos and melodies for better composition.

Guitar lick #1:

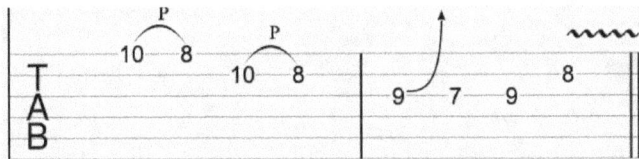

In this first example, we utilize the pull-off at the 10th fret to the 8th fret on the first and second strings. We then add a bend on the 9th fret third string and finish off the lick with a vibrato on the 8th fret second string.

Remember, It's not enough to just run up and down the scales. You want to utilize the techniques necessary to bring them to life and make them sound pleasant to the ear.

48

Guitar lick #2:

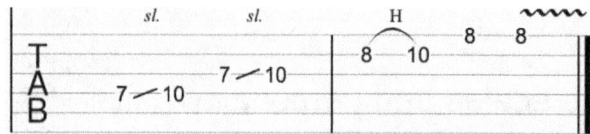

In this example, we slide from the 7th fret to the 10th on the fourth and third strings. We then hammer on from the 8th fret to the 10th on the second string and end the lick with a vibrato on the 8th fret first string.

Guitar Lick #3:

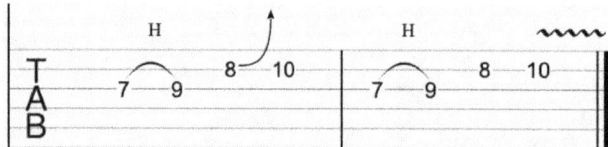

In this last example, we do a repeated lick but change it up a bit. We start with a hammer on the 7th fret to the 9th on the third string, then a bend on the 8th fret, and a 10 on the second string.

The repeated lick is similar, but instead of a bend on the 8th fret second string, we add a vibrato on the 10th fret second string.

Study these licks and see clearly how they come out of the notes in the major pentatonic scale. You can also add the blue note to create new ones.

Lesson 19: Minor scale guitar licks

Now let's look at some basic minor scale guitar licks. These are similar to the major except they use the notes of the minor scale.

As I mentioned before, a simple three or four-note phrase is a great place to start. In the next chapter, we will dive deeper into this concept. But for now, let's get some basics down that we can build our lead guitar playing on.

Guitar lick #1

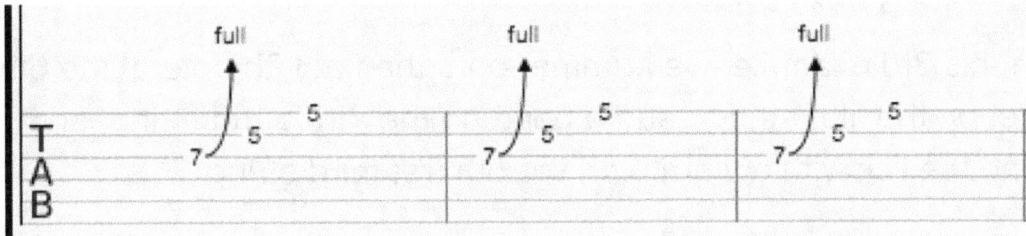

This is the most famous guitar lick of them all. Used by all lead guitar players. I highly recommend you practice it daily until you master it.

In this example, you bend the 7th fret of the third string up and then plat the 5th fret of the second and first strings. Three notes played one right after the other. Very much like a three-letter word to a novelist.

Guitar lick #2:

In this example, we use a pull-off from the 8th fret to the 5th fret on the second string and then pick the 7th fret on the third string, back to the 5th fret on the second string.

Guitar lick #3:

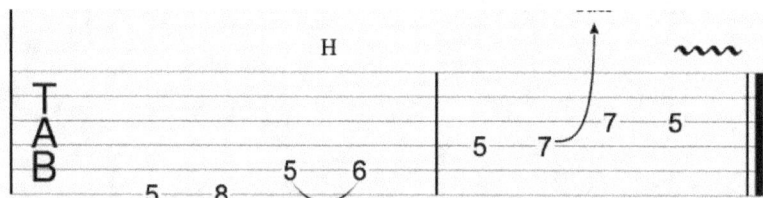

In this 3rd example, we hammer onto the flat fifth note at the 6th fret on the fifth string, add a bend on the 7th fourth string, and end the lick with a vibrato on the 5th fret third string.

These examples show you how to put these techniques together to create lead guitar magic. Study them and put them into practical application.

If you take time to study the fundamentals, you will be able to excel much quicker later down the line. If not, you will notice it when you try to play more complex compositions.

Lesson 20: Chapter 4 Quiz

In Chapter 4 we have learned about the Blues scale, and how it is very similar to the pentatonic. Along with that, we take a look at some guitar licks from the major and minor pentatonic scales.

Once again, a learning assessment is presented for your benefit. To see how well you have learned and retained the information in this lesson.

Q: What note is added to the minor blues scale?

A: _____

Q: What makes it different than the minor pentatonic?

A: _____

Q: How many notes are in the minor blues scale?

A: _____

Q: What are the notes of the A minor blues scale?

A: _____

Q: What two things does this added note do?

A: _____

Q: How many different places can this note be added?

A: _____

Q: This addition adds what to our mindset?

A: _____

Q: This addition adds what to our fingers?

A: _____

Q: What note is added in the major blues scale?

A: _____

Q: What are the notes of the C major blues scale?

A: _____

Q: What notes are in the C major pentatonic scale?

A: _____

Q: What makes the blue note beneficial to the scale?

A: _____

Remember, the development and understanding of these concepts will help improve your understanding of the guitar fretboard and notes in the scales.

Study and practice daily to fully understand their application.

Chapter 4 Summary

In chapter four, we learned about the blues scale, and how it can help enhance our lead guitar playing. By adding a certain note to both the major and minor pentatonic scales.

First, you add the flat 5th note to the minor pentatonic scale. This can be done in two places within it. This addition creates a different shade of color and emotion.

Second, you add the flat 3rd note to the major pentatonic scale. This allows for more flexibility in your playing, as well as creates a different emotion like the minor pentatonic scale.

Third, you have learned about guitar licks that can be played out of the major pentatonic. Add the blue note, and you can use it as well. This is where the rubber begins to meet the road.

Lastly, you learn popular guitar licks that can be made out of the minor pentatonic scale. And just like before, you can add the flat 5th note and create further licks. This is how you bring the scales to life.

Remember, once you get the scale patterns down, you want to start working on your personality traits (hammer-ons, bends, slides, pull-offs, and vibrato) to create solos and melodies.

54

Chapter 5 Additional Techniques

Lesson 21: Soloing with double stops

Another approach to playing solos is with double stops. This is when you play two notes at the same time. Remember, it's how you play the notes that counts.

These are a very common practice in the blues. This allows for a more robust tone as a single guitarist and another way you can approach creating rhythmic melodies.

 Example of double stops:

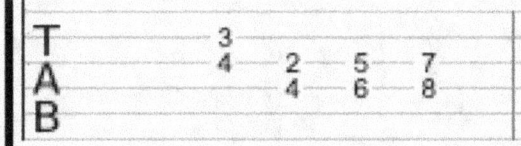

As you can see from this example, two notes are played together. Like regular chords. These are usually on two strings and move up and down the fretboard.

These can be played on two strings next to each other, or a string apart. Either way, many different sounds can be made with them.

Example #2:

```
T----------9--------7--------|-------5--------4-------||
A------9--------7-----------|---6--------5-----------||
B---------------------------|------------------------||
```

In this example, you have two notes that are staggered and skip a string. This means that you would play them one right after another instead of together like in the last example.

Notice how the 9 and 7 are a fret apart, and the 6 and 5 are a fret next to each other. This change in frets keeps them in harmony with each other.

Example #3:

```
T-------7---3---8----|---------------10---13---||
A----5--8---2---7----|--13---16---9----12------||
B----6---------------|--12---15----------------||
```

This example is similar to the first one except they are in different locations and reverse along the fretboard.

Work with these and listen to how they sound. Look for examples of these within the scales that you have previously learned. They are loaded with them.

Just like the other techniques, they will take time to learn and put into application. Take your time and be patient.

Lesson 22: Soloing with octaves

Another technique to use when soloing is octaves. These are two notes that are the same. They can also be used for playing rhythm as well. These reside all over the fretboard.

This application which is similar to the double-stop method is a great way to enrich your sound and add depth to your solos. This is because you are adding another note of the same caliber, just a pitch apart.

Example of octaves:

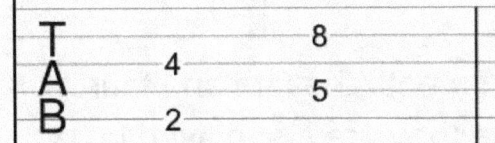

In this example, we have two octaves. One on the 2nd fret fifth string, and one at the 5th fret fourth string.

Notice how the note shifts over one fret on the second octave. This is because of the B string. Make sure to take note of this when playing octaves on the fourth string.

As you learn where different octaves are along the fretboard, you'll begin to see their benefit when it comes to playing melody lines.

Example #2:

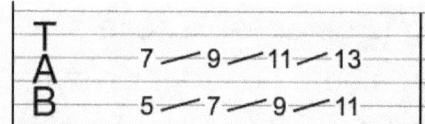

In this example, we have octaves all on the same string. We start at the 5th fret and slide up to the 11th. This can make for a very nice melody line in the right context.

Example #3:

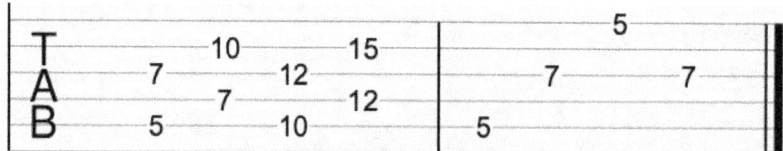

In this example, we have octaves on both the fifth and fourth strings, and in the second measure they are just played in single notes. These are two different approaches to playing octaves.

Octaves are not only a great way to add different shades of color to your solos, but they are also an excellent way to master the fretboard.

I recommend you work on them for these two reasons. The more you know the fretboard, the more you can unlock its mysteries. And believe me, there are many.

Lesson 23: Triplets & repeated licks

Another great way to approach soloing is by utilizing triplets and repeated licks.

Example of triplets:

In this example, we have a sequence of three notes in two measures, which make a nice-sounding melody.

Example #2:

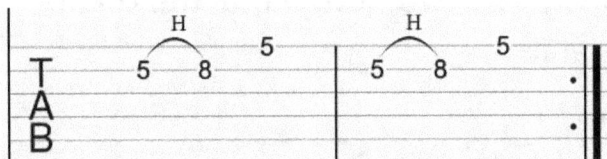

In this example, we utilize a hammer-on at the 5th fret second string and end the triplet on the 5th fret first string. Also notice, that at the end of the measure, we have a new symbol. This is called a repeat sign.

Triplets can sound really cool when repeated several times.

Triplets and repeated licks kind of go together. That is why they are in the same lesson. The difference between the two is that a triplet only uses three notes, as where a repeated lick can use more than three notes.

Either way, both can be highly effective when creating ear-catching melodies. The repeated sequence of notes catches the ear by surprise and can hold the attention of the listener.

Example #3:

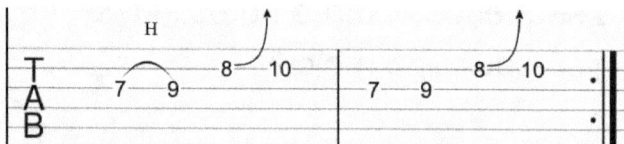

 In this example, we have a lick of four notes. Utilizing both the hammer-on and a string bend. The two note bar at the end of the measure tells us to repeat it.

Example 4:

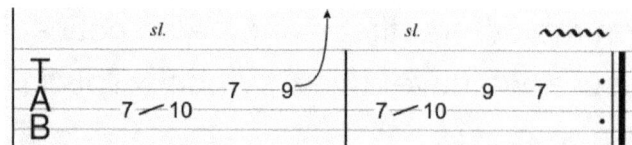

This example uses a slide, a bend, and a vibrato. Practice these daily, and create your own triplets and repeated licks.

Lesson 24: Developing finger strength

Now that we know some basic principles of lead guitar playing, scales, personality traits, and guitar licks, we can focus on developing finger strength. Finger exercises are best for this.

Let's take a look at a few.

Exercise #1:

In this example, we start on the 5th fret first string and proceed to the 8th. Use all four fingers. Index on 5, middle on 6, ring on 7, and pinky on 8. Then continue this through all six strings.

Exercise #2:

This example is similar except you start on the open E and proceed through the rest of the strings.

Remember, make sure to use all four fingers in these exercises. This will help not only build finger strength, but it will also build finger independence.

Exercise #3:

In this example, we do an exercise across four strings. Starting on the 2nd fret first string. Then use the index finger again, to descend in the opposite direction. This exercise gives you a chance to utilize all of the fretboard.

Exercise #4:

This example is similar to the first one, but you start on the 6th string and change up the order. Still using all four fingers as before, and utilizing all six strings.

These exercises will help to develop finger strength, independence, and enhanced fretboard knowledge. But for this to happen, they must be practiced daily. I recommend doing them as a warm-up to more advanced techniques.

Lesson 25: Chapter 5 Quiz

In this chapter, we have learned more techniques that can be used for lead guitar phrasing. These will allow you to make your solos sound like music.

Q: What are double stops?

A: _____

Q: How many strings do they use?

A: _____

Q: Where are they located on the fretboard?

A: _____

Q: What are octaves?

A: _____

Q: How are octaves different from double stops?

A: _____

Q: Where do octaves reside?

A: _____

Q: How far apart are octaves along the fretboard?

A: _____

Q: In example 2, what technique are octaves using?

A: _____.

Q: Octaves are a great way to do what to your playing?

A: _____

Q: What are triplets?

A: _____

Q: The two-dot symbol at the end of the measure mean?

A: _____

Q: What is the best way to develop finger strength?

A: _____

Q: Along with finger strength, what else can be developed?

A: _____

Q: How many fingers should be used in these exercises?

A: _____

Q: Are all 6 strings used, or just some of them?

A: _____

This chapter gives you a foundation of musical knowledge, along with techniques that will enhance your lead playing.

Chapter 5 Summary

In this chapter, we have looked at a great way to add a new sound to the triad. This is done by adding the flat 7th note of the scale. This will create a dominant 7th chord.

The 7th chord is a very common chord type and must be added to your chord vocabulary. These chord types will allow you to create a different type of emotion than their major and minor counterparts.

By understanding how these chords are created and being able to find the correct note, within the key they come from, you will be able to increase your knowledge of music.

Don't forget that these chords can be easily formed if you know where your notes are on the fretboard. That is why it is vitally important to know your notes on each string.

The G7 chord just moves the note on the first string two frets down. While the D7 chord just flips itself backward from the D major chord.

Remember, the major 7th chord will just add the natural 7th note to the major triad, and the minor 7th chord will add the flat.

Chapter 6 Major Minor Theory

Lesson 26: C major A minor

The major-minor theory is when two scales share the same notes,   and this is what makes them relative. It's the understanding of this relationship that will allow you to move between two different scales and stay on key.

Let's look at the notes of two scales to see why this relationship works and is beneficial.

Notes of C major: C D E F G A B C
Notes of A minor: A B C D E F G A

As we can see, these two scales share the same notes. The only difference is that the major starts on C and the minor starts on A.

Why is this important you ask?

Because it allows you to switch between scales and stay in key. Knowing about this relationship between the two scales allows you to play in either C major, or A minor and switch between the two at any time.

Chord creation:

C major = 1 3 5 = C E G

You can also create an A minor chord.

A minor = 1 b3 5 = A C E

Since both of these chords are in these two scales, you can easily switch between them in a chord progression.

This is why the minor pentatonic and the major pentatonic are right next to each other. This position allows you to switch between them easily while staying in key.

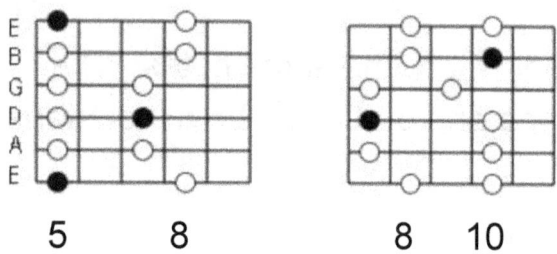

The first pattern at the 5th fret is A minor, and the second pattern at the 8th fret is C major. Since the two scales are relative, you can switch between them when you solo, and stay in key.

Lesson 27: G major E minor

These two scales are relative also. Why? Because they are made of the same notes. Just like the last two scales we looked at.

Notes of G major: G A B C D E F# G
Notes of E minor: E F# G A B C D E

Once again like before, we can see that the two scales have the same notes, and this makes them relative.

The major scale starts on the G note, and the minor scale starts on the E note. Even though they are two different scales, they are made up of the same notes.

This knowledge enables you to create chord progressions that can enhance your ability to compose and arrange solos that fit seamlessly over them.

By understanding the difference between the bright uplifting tones of the major scale, and the moody somber tones of the minor, you can create a wide variety of musical landscapes.

Chord creation:

In addition to creating the G major chord and the E minor chord, you can also create others, if you understand this concept.

G major = 1 3 5 = G B D
E minor = 1 b3 5 = E G B

When creating chords to solo over, always start with the triads. The 1 3 & 5th notes of the scale.

G major = G A B C D E F# G
           1 2 3 4 5 6 7 8

Start with the A note you get: A C E = A minor
Start with the B note you get: B D F# = B minor
Start with the C note you get: C E G = C major
Start with the D note you get: D F# A = D major.

By going in a sequence of 1 3 5, you get a lot of different chords out of the scale. This is helpful to know when creating compositions and soloing over them.

I recommend you study and practice this concept.

Lesson 28: D major B minor

These are also common keys to solo over. D major, and its relative minor, the B minor.

Why are they relative?

Because they are made up of the same notes. This must not be confused with the D minor. Which would be a different set of notes.

D major: D E F# G A B C# D
D minor: D E F G A Bb C D

If you look at these two keys, you can see they are not of the same notes. This means the relative keys are different as well. Remember, the relative major or minor, will have the same note.

D major: D E F# G A B C# D
B minor: B C# D E F# G A B

Since the D minor above has different notes than the D major, it is not a relative minor. The relative minor to the D major is the B minor because it has the same notes.

The relative minor (which will always be the 6th tone degree in the major scale) will always have the same notes as the major that it comes out of.

Since D major and B minor have the same notes, we can easily move between them and stay in key when soloing.

B minor: D major

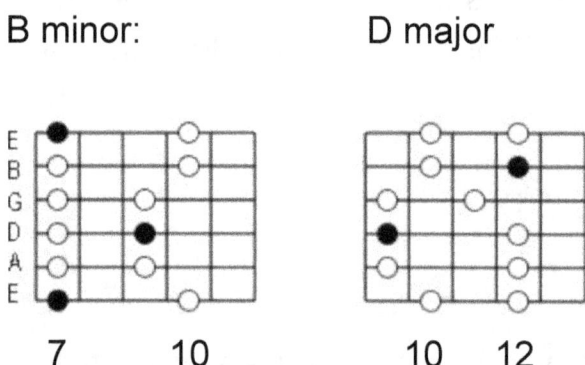

   7   10   10   12

Just like before, these two pentatonic patterns line up to show this work. The first pattern played at the 7th fret will be in the key of B minor. The second pattern played at the 10th fret will be in the key of D major.

By knowing this, you can easily switch between these two patterns when soloing and staying in key. Why? Because they are made up of the same notes.

Lesson 29: A major F# minor

Now let's look at our next common key for soloing, A major and its relative minor F#. Why F# and not F? Because the note F is sharpened in the key of A major. Remember, the major scale needs to have the Do Re Mi sound to it.

A major scale = A B C# D E F# G# A

You will hear the Do Re Mi if you go through these notes on your fretboard. It wouldn't sound correct if you were to change any of the notes (for example: F# to F).

The minor scale doesn't have to have that sound, but the major does. By training our ears to hear this in the notes, we can determine which notes need to be played within any major scale.

A major: A B C# D E F# G# A
F# minor: F# G# A B C# D E F#

Once again, the A and the F# at the end of the scales just move you into the next octave. So technically, you only have 7 notes in the scales.

74

Chord creation:

Just like before with the other scales, knowing the notes allows us the create chords and chord progressions to solo over.

A major: 1 3 5 = A C# E
B minor: 1 b3 5 = B D F#
C# minor: 1 b3 5 = C# E G#
D major: 1 3 5 = D F# A
E amjor: 1 3 5 = E G# B

Notice how there is a note in between each of these chords. This makes them easy to figure out. Remember, a triad is a three-note chord.

Major triad = 1 3 5
Minor triad = 1 b3 5

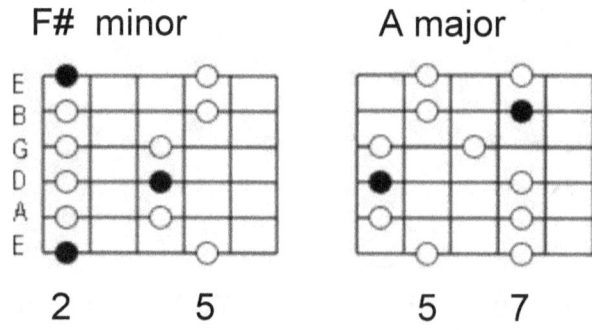

Can you see how the pentatonic scale positions work the same as the other lessons? This is what makes them highly effective.

Lesson 30: Chapter 6 Quiz

In this chapter, we have learned some vital information or relative major minor theory that can help out playing solos.

Q: What does it mean when two scales share the same notes?

A: _____

Q: What is the relative minor of C major?

A: _____

Q: What is the relative major of E minor?

A: _____

Q: What is the relative minor of D major?

A: _____

Q: What chords can be created out of G major?

A: _____

Q: Why is this information important to know?

A: _____

Q: How can it help out your lead guitar playing?

A: _____

Chapter 6 Summary

In this chapter, we have learned about relative major minor theory. When two scales share the same notes.

First, we look at C major. A great place to start because it has no sharps or flats. When we take the A minor scale, we can see that it consists of the same notes. j

This means that if you were in the key of C major, you could solo in the key of C major, or you could solo in the key of A minor, as they share the same notes.

This concept works not only for the other scales presented but all 12 in the musical alphabet. Find the notes to any major scale, and see which one is the relative minor.

Lastly, we learn about how we can form chords out of the notes within the scales. This is also important to know as it helps not only lead guitar playing but also with songwriting.

Chapter 7 Basic Scale Theory

Lesson 31: The major scale

When it comes to scale theory, it all starts with the 12 notes of the musical alphabet. This is also called the chromatic scale, and out of these 12 notes, we take 7 and get the major scale.

Let's look at this in more detail.

It all starts with the musical alphabet. The twelve notes that go from A to G#. **A A# B C C# D D# E F F# G G#.**
                               1 2 3 4 5 6 7 8 9 10 11 12

Out of these 12 notes, we take 7 to make the major scale.

These aren't just any notes, they are notes of a certain interval. An interval is the distance between two notes.

A note of 1 fret distance (for example, A to A#) is called a half step, and a 2 fret distance is called a whole step.

Half step = 1 fret (A-A#)
Whole step = 2 frets (A-B)

This can be very beneficial to know because it allows us to come up with a scientific formula of whole steps and help steps that work for the major scale.

This will allow us to easily figure out what notes consist in any major scale. Let's look at an example.

Whole step, half step example:

```
C   D   E   F   G   A   B   C
1   2   3   4   5   6   7   8
  W   W   H   W   W   W H
```

As you can see from the example above, the scientific formula for the major scale is **W-W-W-W-W-W-H.**

*The 8th note is the same as the first and it completes the scale by coming around to the first. But there are only 7 individual notes in the major scale.

If we follow this example with the G major scale, we can see what notes are needed.

```
G major = 1   2   3   4   5   6   7   8
            W   W   H   W   W   W H
          G   A   B   C   D   E   F# G
```

This formula works with all the major scales that we have learned so far.

D major = D   E   F#   G   A   B   C#   D
    1   2   3   4   5   6   7   8
    W   W   H   W   W   W   H

A major = A   B   C#   D   E   F#   G   A
    1   2   3   4   5   6   7   8
    W   W   H   W   W   W   H

E major = E   F#   G#   A   B   C#   D#   E
    1   2   3   4   5   6   7   8
    W   W   H   W   W   W   H

B major = B   C#   D#   E   F#   G#   A#   B
    1   2   3   4   5   6   7   8
    W   W   H   W   W   W   H

As you can see, all these major scales are made up of the same whole-step half-step formula. Also, if you go through the notes, you'll hear how they all have the sound of;
Do Re Mi Fa So La Ti Do.

Lesson 32: The minor scale

Now that we have an idea about how the major scale is created, we can take a look at the minor scale.

As we learned in the last chapter, it can be very beneficial to know about the minor scale. Not only for major minor theory but also because of the emotion that it creates.

To make a major scale into a minor scale, you flatten the 3rd, 6th, and 7th notes of the scale.

Minor scale example:

A major = A B C# D E F# G# A
            1 2 3 4 5 6 7 8
         W W H W W W H

A minor = A B C D E F G A
          1 2 b3 4 5 b6 b7 8
        W H W W H W W

Notice how the notes change when we flatten the 3rd, 6th, and 7th notes of the major scale, along with the whole-step half-step formula. Make sure to master this concept. It will help you in lead guitar playing tremendously.

Lesson 33: The melodic minor scale

In addition to creating the natural minor scale, we can also create other minor scales. Like the melodic minor.

The melodic minor scale is similar to the natural minor, except you only need to flatten the 3rd note.

A minor = A B C D E F G A
               1 2 b3 4 5 b6 b7 8

A melodic minor = A B C D E F# G# A
                    1 2 b3 4 5 6 7 8

By flattering only the 3rd note and keeping the 6th and 7th natural, you create a different type of scale.

This can be done with all of the natural minor scales. By flattening only the third, you can create new melodic shades of color.

I recommend you try this out with the other minor scales that you have learned to see how the two scales differ in tone and soundscape.

Lesson 34: The harmonic minor scale

By altering the notes of the minor scale more, we can create another type of minor scale. The harmonic minor scale.

In this minor scale, we only flatten the 3rd and the 6th. This leaves the 7th note natural.

A melodic minor = A B C D E F# G# A
                  1 2 b3 4 5 6 7 8

A harmonic minor = A B C D E F G# A
                  1 2 b3 4 5 b6 7 8

By flattening the 6th and keeping the 7th natural, you create a step and a half. Which is a three-fret distance. It is this distance that gives it character and makes it different than the minor, and the melodic minor.

By knowing the notes of any major scale, you can create three minor scales that all have a different note characteristic to them. This allows you to enhance your creativity and increase your knowledge of music theory.

I recommend you go through the major scales that you have learned in the previous lessons and figure these other minor scales out.

Lesson 35: Chapter 7 Quiz

In this chapter, we look at some basic scale theory. Major, minor, melodic, and harmonic.

Q: What are the 12 notes of the music alphabet?

A: _____

Q: What is another name for the musical alphabet?

A: _____

Q: How many notes make up the major scale?

A: _____

Q: What's the whole-step half-step formula for the major scale?

A: _____

Q: What is the note formula for the minor scale?

A: _____

Q: What is the note formula for the melodic minor scale?

A: _____

Q: What is the note formula for the harmonic minor scale?

A: _____

Study this chapter well as it will help improve your playing.

Chapter 7 Summary

In this chapter, we have looked at the basics of scale theory. This knowledge can help to improve your musicianship and overall understanding of your guitar fretboard.

First, we take a look at the 12 notes that make up the musical alphabet. We also learn that this is also called the chromatic scale. These 12 notes are where all scales come from.

We then look at the 7 notes that make up the major scale. Along with that, we learn about the whole-step half-step note formula. W-W-H-W-W-W-H. This will help you to find the notes of any major scale.

After that, we learn about what needs to be done to make the minor scale. This is important to know because the two scales create different emotions. The major scale creates a happy sound, and the minor is a more somber one.

Lastly, we learn about the melodic and harmonic minor scales. These allow you to expand your fretboard knowledge, and your musical soundscape. Plus enhance your creativity.

Chapter 8: Additional Training

Lesson 36: Develop playing by ear

Aside from learning theory and how to read notation, you also want to work on the art of playing by ear. This is a great skill to have and daily practice will help you to develop it.

It will give you the ability not to have to depend on sheet music or notation of any kind. It also enhances the connection you make with your guitar.

The better connection you make with the instrument, the better guitarist you will become over time.

Tips for playing by ear:

1. Start by going through your scales one note after the other. This will help you with note intervals and pitch recognition. Do this daily for the best results.

2. Play a few notes of a scale and then try to hum the pitch of the next note. Continue this through the rest of the scale. This will also help your ear to hear the pitch of the next note.

3. Work at actively listening to what a piece of music is saying in its chords and melodies. Start with something simple and try to play what you are hearing.

4. Learning to understand basic music theory can help in this area as well. Scale note intervals along with chord voicings can give insight into what to listen for.

5. Take your time and be patient. As it will take time to be efficient at playing songs by ear. Perseverance and dedication are what is needed to develop this skill.

6. Be consistent with your practice. I recommend daily. Learning by ear is a slow process in the beginning. But if you are determined to get it accomplished you will.

7. Last but not least, practice these things daily. The more you apply yourself. The quicker you will see results. Be consistent in your efforts and have fun.

Learning to play by ear is not always easy. But if you stick with it and practice these tips daily, slowly but surely it will develop.

But for that to happen, you must have a genuine passion for music and the persistence to get better at playing your guitar.

Lesson 37: Improvising within a song

Another skill that you want to master, is the art of improvising within a song. This is a journey that can be quite fun to take. It allows your individuality to engage dynamically with the music.

Mastering this skill can not only be fun to develop but also enhance your fretboard knowledge and musical creativity.

Here are some improvisation tips:

1. Make sure that you know all five pentatonic patterns and can be able to play them in any key along the fretboard.

2. Determine what key the song is in that you are going to be soloing over. It'll be either major or minor.

3. Pay attention to the cadence of the rhythm in the song. This will help you to develop a matching melody line.

4. Work on your phrasing, dynamics, and most importantly, staying in key. This is where mastering the intervals of the scales and being able to move within them along the fretboard will come in.

Master the art of improvising through daily practice. Over time you will find your musical voice and style.

Lesson 38: Developing a practice routine

A practice routine will help you track progress, stay focused, and ensure the best use of your time.

Tips for developing a practice routine:

1. Establish goals with daily, weekly, and monthly objectives that define exactly what you want to accomplish.

2. Work daily at accomplishing these goals. Work on techniques that are going to get you there.

3. Structure your practice sessions. Write out exactly what you want to work on and allocate the proper time to each task.

4. Track your daily progress. This will give you a clear picture of what is working and what still needs to be improved.

5. Celebrate milestones that you accomplish. Even small ones. This will keep you inspired and motivated.

Keep it loose and have fun. Practice should never be a chore. It should be something you look forward to daily and feel good about doing.

Lesson 39: Learning solos from recordings

The best way to learn how to compose guitar solos is to learn ones from recordings of your favorite players.

Tips on learning solos from recordings:

1. Pick a simple solo to start. Only a few notes. One that has a melody you can hum.

2. Listen to it over and over, and try to distinguish the intervals between the notes.

3. Listen for the phrasing techniques being used and the cadence of the rhythm.

4. When working with a longer solo, break it down into small sections and link them together as you progress.

5. Use technology to slow the solo down and loop sections as you learn them. This also helps with ear training.

   These tips and techniques will not only help you to learn solos effectively, but deepen your connection with your guitar, and enhance your overall musicianship.

Have patience, persistence, and practice daily.

Lesson 40: Chapter 8 Quiz

In this last chapter, we have learned some training tips that will help us to enjoy the musical journey.

Q: What does it mean to play by ear?
A: _____

Q: How will playing by ear benefit you?
A: _____

Q: What does it mean to improvise within a song?
A: _____

Q: Why purpose does developing a practice routine serve?
A: _____

Q: What is beneficial about learning solos from recordings?
A: _____

Q: Why is all this additional training so important?
A: _____

Remember, these learning assessments are for your benefit. Don't take them lightly, as they will help you to see what you've retained and what still needs to be learned.

Chapter 8 Summary

This final chapter is presented to give you insight into what can take your playing to the next level.

But for you to do that, you must apply what you have learned daily. Just like all the other lessons in this training.

First, we look at what it takes to develop playing by ear. In this lesson, you are given tips that can help to accomplish this.

Then we look at mastering the art of improvisation. This is where you create original solos and melody lines.

We then look at developing a practice routine. This application will help you to excel at a more efficient rate.

Last but not least, you look at how to learn solos from recordings. This skill can benefit you in composition and improvisation.

If you work on these techniques, and add them to your daily routine, you will enhance your knowledge of the fretboard, rhythm, and timing, as well as a better understanding of music in general.

Learn To Play Lead Guitar Conclusion

If you've made it this far I congratulate you on your accomplishments and say "Thank you for your purchase of this book and your time learning to play the guitar". You seem like the kind of student that I'd love to teach in person.

This training has taught you many things about playing lead guitar, and you should now be well-versed in many techniques and concepts related to it.

As well as a basic foundation of music in general. But to fully understand it all, you need to study, practice, and apply what you have learned. This can only be accomplished through a daily committed dedication to the guitar.

Learning to play lead guitar is an exciting journey. With effort, discipline, and persistence, you can develop your inner musical expression. Through this activity, you will reach the culmination of your learning desires.

Understanding scales and what keys to play them in is just for starters. You must go further in understanding how the notes and techniques within them paint a musical picture, and how chords work to solo over.

Remember, there is still much more to learn about playing lead guitar, as this book doesn't cover everything. If that was the case, it would be the size of an encyclopedia. But what it does offer, will allow you to build a solid foundation to expand on.

Make sure to embrace the process. Enjoy the journey. Be patient and allow time for your mind and muscles to develop. Once you do, you'll discover a whole new world, and enjoy the commitment you've made to your guitar.

Follow this guide as instructed step-by-step, and if you have any questions about any lessons in the book, be sure to let me know. I will be happy to assist you in any way I can. My way of saying thank you for your purchase.

And, if you feel private lessons might help you learn the language of music better, be sure to contact me and we'll set up a free consultation.

Visit my website at DwaynesGuitarLessons.com.

Best of luck, practice daily, and most of all, have fun.

Sincerely, Dwayne Jenkins

Other Titles That Can Help You Progress

Learn To Play Rhythm Guitar

A comprehensive training guide that will help you to master the art of playing rhythm guitar. No matter if you are just getting started, or have been playing for years. This book can help.

Easy step-by-step lessons that go through the fundamental principles that allow you to build a solid foundation and get ready to play lead guitar.

How To Play Guitar Modes:

Guitar modes are another aspect of playing lead guitar.
Different from the pentatonic, these come out of the major scale
and offer a different approach to playing solos and melodies.

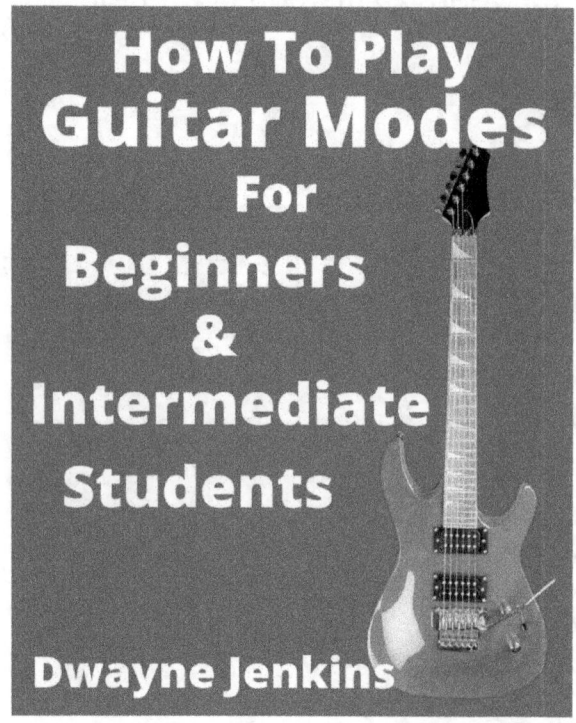

Guitar modes are a great way to master the fretboard as well as
get a better understanding of scale theory and advanced
techniques. A comprehensive study guide that will take your
playing and musicianship to the next level.

Learn Guitar Chord Theory:

Learn Guitar Chord Theory presents you with the fundamental principles necessary to understand in a simple formula, the inner workings of guitar chords.

A comprehensive study guide with step-by-step lessons designed to enhance your knowledge of the guitar fretboard, and increase your guitar chord vocabulary.

All books are authored by Dwayne Jenkins, published by Tritone Publishing, and available worldwide.

Digital formats of all titles are also available for quicker learning. Just download it onto your computer and start learning right away.

Self-study is a great way to learn as it allows you to not only go at your own pace but also develop the skills of self-discipline and time management. Which can benefit you in other areas of your life.

Also, be sure to check out Dwayne's Guitar Lessons video channel on YouTube. These are free lessons that cover a wide variety of topics related to playing guitar.

No matter if you are working on rhythm, lead, theory, or even working on guitar maintenance, it is all here in these lessons. Which are available 24 hours a day, 7 days a week, 365 days a year.

Best of luck, and have fun

About the Author

Dwayne Jenkins is a professional guitar teacher, an accomplished musician, and an entrepreneur. He has been learning, playing, and teaching guitar lessons throughout Denver, CO for over two decades.

He is now bringing his special training skills and methodology that have been honed and hand-crafted throughout the years on how to play to students around the world.

Dwayne has a unique exciting approach that gets students of all ages and skill levels enjoying the fun of playing guitar and ukulele. His enthusiasm and love for teaching shine through with every lesson that he creates.

His lessons are designed to enhance your ability to progress. No matter your reason for learning, there will always be something in Dwayne's books and products to help you achieve your dreams.

So if you're a student looking to start, or a student looking to further your education, be sure to get involved with Dwayne's guitar lessons and learn what so many people have already discovered why learning to play the guitar, is one of the greatest things you can do for yourself.

100

What Students Are Saying About Dwayne's Guitar Lessons

"Dwayne, thank you so much for everything you have taught me and done for me. You are an amazing guitarist and wonderful teacher" BJ.

"Dwayne, it has been a true pleasure to have you at our house each week! Ken & Trevor have learned so much through you and your teachings. Thank you!" Lisa.

"Dwayne, thank you for being a great teacher and teaching me many great songs. This is a skill that will last me a lifetime." Danielle.

"Dwayne, we want you to know we are honored to have you at the studio. We appreciate all that you do and are grateful that we can leave you in charge" Angie & Wilson M.E.C.

"Dwayne, we are so glad you are our Teacher. It's been three years already can you believe it? Thank you again. You're the best!" Chelsey & Lucas.

"Dwayne, we are so glad that you are in our lives. Chelsey & Lucas enjoy their time with you and look up to you. Looking forward to another great year!" Love and best wishes, Ken & Sue.

"Dwayne, thank you so much for being not only an awesome guitar teacher, but an awesome friend as well" Kayla.

"Dwayne, thank you so much for all the years of doing lessons. You have been very patient with my progress helped me to build confidence in myself and inspired me to follow my dreams. And in doing so you have become a great friend" Jake.

"Dwayne, thank you for teaching Nick guitar so well. He loves it and is getting quite good fast. I'm amazed!" Jane.

"Dwayne, Thank you so much for teaching me every Saturday and not only teaching me guitar but also about life and helping me with setting my goals. You are a great teacher, mentor, and the best friend ever" Carson.

"There is not another person I would want to be teaching me a guitar! His 1 on 1 teaching makes learning guitar very personal & exhilarating. He teaches at your pace and takes pride in what YOU want to learn. The best part...if Dwayne doesn't know a song a student wants to play, he takes time out of the week to learn it His teaching comes to life in my performance and has progressed over the last 8 years. Words cannot describe how amazing a teacher, rockstar, and true friend Dwayne has become to me" Dominic.

104